Richard Nicholson
Open to Question

Starters for discussion and role-play

Edward Arnold

1978 Richard Nicholson

First published in Great Britain 1978 by
Edward Arnold (Publishers) Ltd
41 Bedford Square
London WC1B 3DQ

Edward Arnold (Australia) Pty Ltd
80 Waverley Road
Caulfield East
Victoria 3145
Australia

Reprinted 1979, 1984

All Rights Reserved. No part of this publication may be reproduced, stored in a retrieval system, or transmitted in any form or by any means, electronic, mechanical, photocopying, recording or otherwise, without the prior permission of Edward Arnold (Publishers) Ltd.

British Library Cataloguing in Publication Data

Nicholson, Richard
   Open to question.
   1. Social psychology
   I. Title
   301.1   HM251

ISBN 0-7131-0186-5

Designed by Clive Barnes of DP Press Ltd, Sevenoaks
Typeset by Type Practitioners Ltd, Sevenoaks
Printed and bound by Spottiswoode Ballantyne, Colchester and London.

Contents

Family Matters   6

People at Risk   14

Group Life   20

Power and Authority   28

Man and Beast   36

Communicators and Persuaders   42

Questions of Belief   50

The Future   58

Acknowledgements

The Publisher's thanks are due to the following for permission to reproduce copyright material:

John Murray Ltd for John Betjeman's poem 'Harvest Hymn' from *Collected Poems*; Hamish Hamilton Ltd for Paul Dehn's 'Gutter Press' from *The Fern on the Rock*,© Dehn Enterprises 1965, 1976; *Evening Gazette*, Cleveland for the article 'Parents Warned on Child Sterilization'; Faber & Faber Ltd for an extract from Thom Gunn's 'Klaus von Stauffenberg' from *My Sad Captains*, Ted Hughes' 'The Jaguar' from *The Hawk in the Rain*, Edwin Muir's 'The Horses' from *Collected Poems* and Stephen Spender's 'My parents kept me from children who were rough' from *Collected Poems*; E.P. Dutton for an extract from John Holt's *Freedom and Beyond*; Country Life for Ada Jackson's poem 'Our Brother Richard'; Jonathan Cape for Robert Frost's poem 'Out, Out' from *The Poetry of Robert Frost*, ed. E.C. Lathem; Peter Porter for his poem 'Your Attention Please' and Granada Publishing Ltd and Rupert Hart-Davies MacGibbon for R.S. Thomas' 'In Church' from *Pieta*.

Our thanks are due to the following for advertisements on the pages shown below:

The Advertising Standards Authority Ltd, p. 48; Beecham Proprietaries, p. 48; Columbia Warner Distributors Ltd, p. 46; Health Education Council, p. 48; Imperial Tobacco Ltd, p. 48; New Realm Films, p. 46; Save the Children Fund, p. 18 and United Artists, p. 46.

Our thanks are also due to the following for permission to reproduce copyright photographs:

P.A.F. International (6, 17, 20 bottom left); Shelter (7, 34); Sheelah Latham and Ron Chapman (10, 20 top left and right, 21 left); Tony Othen (11); Invalid Children's Aid Association (14); Save the Children Fund (18); Rex Features (20 middle left and bottom right, 28, 50); Popperfoto (21 right); Keystone Press (22, 40, 53); Henry Grant (24); John Walmsley (30); Central Office of Information (32); Associated Press and Campaign for Nuclear Disarmament (33); John Herbert (36); Syndication International (37); Camera Press (38, 39, 44, 55, 60/61); BBC copyright photograph (42); Mansell Collection (54); Space Frontiers (58, 63); U.S. Air Force (62).

Introduction

Open to Question starts from the premise that it is at least as important to develop opinions and value-judgements as it is to acquire knowledge. Students in school and college are often given a passive role as learners; the use of this book should encourage students to become more active.

The book is intended for use by students between the ages of fourteen and eighteen in any area of the curriculum where the teacher feels the discussion of value-issues is appropriate. It may also prove helpful in the time provided in many schools for tutors to undertake 'pastoral work' with their groups. I do not see discussion and role-play as a subject area (confined to English, or drama, or work in the humanities) but as a teaching-learning method available to all teachers across the curriculum.

The word 'starters' is used advisedly. This book is deliberately open-ended, hopefully encouraging teachers and students to go on developing ideas in their own ways. The book tries to pay students the compliment of believing that they should, and can, handle controversial material and real-life issues in a mature way, and I know this to be true from my own experience. Some 'practical' work is included because some students may become frustrated by discussion which apparently does not 'lead anywhere', and because the activities are seen as valuable in themselves. The book suggests an approach which can be adapted and extended as the teacher pleases. It is easy to see how prose literature, for instance, could be used to supplement the material provided: for example passages describing different experiences in various fictional schools would be helpful to the discussion of questions raised in chapter 4.

Open to Question probably leaves more to the teacher (and group) than most classroom books. The material is deliberately 'adult' and provocative, and if, at first sight, it appears to raise rather stark, black and white issues, the teacher can, by skilful chairmanship, help the group to appreciate the various shades of grey. I recommend that the teacher uses this material to try to draw out the views of the group without seeking to preach or proselytise, but each teacher will no doubt decide his own role in discussion. If the teacher is too obtrusive in role-play he will probably defeat the object of the method. The material is designed to throw the student back on his own resources; to make him think for himself.

Understandably some teachers are tentative about attempting role-play and drama. The role-play suggested here is a 'problem-solving approach' which can arise naturally from discussion. My advice to the teacher inexperienced in this approach is to move unobtrusively from discussion into role-play without obviously signalling that 'role-play has now begun'. The

'Situations' in each chapter can be discussed without role-play but role-play usually adds a good deal to the insights gained by students and their ability to 'empathise'. The group can add further situations to those suggested, and many of the ideas within each chapter could usefully be developed in role-play although this is not always stated specifically.

The word 'group' is used rather than class. It is intended that the book could be used in a number of different ways, by a class or by a small group, with or without the teacher present. Discussion usually works best when students can make eye-contact in a circle or hollow square formation, and the teacher may want to join the group in a physical sense rather than remaining aloof on the dais!

Picture starters
There are some very striking photographs in this book and they, too, can be used as starters for discussion and, in some cases, role-play as well. The group's initial discussion will probably be helped if the following questions are considered:

1. What is the main focus of interest in the picture?
2. The picture is a frozen moment of time. Imagine it now as a 'still' from a film or part of real life. What would have happened before this moment and what will happen after it?
3. Again imagine your picture as a 'still' from a film. Discuss what sound track would accompany the pictures. What are the sounds we can hear?
4. Now think of the other senses. They may not be relevant in the case of every picture, but consider smell, taste, and touch (textures) as far as they do apply.
5. How do you think the photographer wanted you to feel when you looked at the picture?
6. How *do* you feel when you look at it?
7. Does the picture remind you of anything else? Does it remind you of something that has happened to you or something you have read about, or seen on television or on film or in a dream?
8. Does it now suggest a situation or incident or story-line which could be developed in role-play or drama?

Finally, I would like to thank students from the Sheraton Comprehensive School in Stockton-on-Tees for contributing some of the ideas included in this book, and to emphasise once again that the group itself will often offer the best growing point for discussion.

R.N.

Family Matters

Trouble and strife?
The dilemma of a battered wife...

The scene is a darkened television studio. The lighting is arranged so that Morag, who doesn't want to be recognised, sits in silhouette while the interviewer can be seen.

Int: When did your husband first use violence against you?
Morag: Not until the first child came along. We had rows before that but he never hit me.
Int: Why do you think the violence started?
Morag: Well, it didn't happen often at first but when the baby cried a lot it got on my husband's nerves and sometimes he took it out on me. It happened more as we had more children. By the time the third came along it was happening more often.
Int: What form did the violence take?
Morag: Well, you know, hitting me with his fist ... in the face and about the body sometimes. I bruise easily and it got difficult to explain it away. My mother soon realised what was happening. She kept telling me to leave my husband.
Int: Did you?
Morag: Quite often. I would leave home and take the kids to my mother's, but I'd return, usually after two or three days.
Int: Why, if things were so bad?
Morag: I don't know. I suppose because I loved him. I haven't stopped loving him really, even now.
Int: Even when he was so brutal towards you?
Morag: He couldn't seem to help himself. At times he could be quite affectionate and considerate, especially if I was ever ill ... and he never hit the children.
Int: Was it always the children who drove him to be violent towards you?
Morag: No, if he was very worried or tired. If things at work were getting on top of him. Any kind of worry or stress made him lose his temper and then he'd lash out. Then he'd regret it afterwards. Where some men would just argue and shout he'd sooner or later have to use his fists.
Int: What finally made you break with your husband and go to the hostel?*
Morag: The attacks got worse and the children were growing up. I didn't think it was right for them to see such things. There was one time when he broke my nose and I told him that if he ever hit me again I'd leave him for good. Nothing happened for a long period. I think he was scared himself by how violent he'd been that last time. Then one night we had a row because he'd left his job — a

* Refuges for battered wives exist up and down the country and are run by Women's Aid groups. They can be found through social services departments, the police, the Samaritans, or Citizens' Advice Bureaux.

very good job — because of a disagreement with his boss. He hit me in the end and then dragged me out of the kitchen door and locked me out. A neighbour called the Police. I'd heard of the hostel by then and I went straight round there. I've been there for two months now.

Int: How do you feel about the hostel?

Morag: The people who run it are marvellous. It's given me a breathing space, but I don't know in the long run. I don't like to think of the children growing up without a home of their own . . . in an institution, sort of . . .

Int: Why did you choose the hostel on thi occasion rather than go to your parents home?

Morag: Well, I couldn't stay with my parent for any long period. They've only a small bungalow and with three kids i would be too much for them.

Int: How do you see the future?

Morag: I don't know. I might return to my hus band. He wants me to go back. I think children need a home and a father. Bu then I'm afraid it would all start again if I went back. And perhaps I've beer partly to blame . . .

▶ Discuss Morag's dilemma. What should she do? What is best for the children?

Why do you think some men are violent towards their wives? Do Morag's reasons sound convincing? Do you think the wife is often partly to blame?

What do you think of hostels as an answer to the problem? Can you think of any other answer?

▶ Serious rows between parents can be alarming to their children. Should parents always hide their disagreements?

What are the most common causes of rows between husband and wife?

Is there anything children can do to help relations between their parents?

How difficult is it for a man to understand the kind of life his wife leads, and vice versa?

Love and marriage ?

Dear Meg...
Your problems answered with wisdom and sensitivity

Dear Meg,

I've discovered that my wife is having an affair with a man I thought was a good friend. This is the third affair that I know of in our fifteen years of marriage and after the last one I said that if it happened again I would sue for a divorce. I love my wife and would not wish to saddle myself or my children with all the problems of a one-parent family. Should I try to shock her out of her selfishness by having an affair myself? Should I blame myself for her apparent need to find happiness with other men? Should I make a clean break this time or allow her to continue with her affair and live at home in the hope that it will blow over? I feel at the end of my tether and desperate for advice.

A.J.
Birmingham.

▶ Your group runs the 'Dear Meg' Problem page. Discuss the kind of reply you are going to give to A.J.

▶ Discuss the wider issues raised by this letter:

Is fidelity necessary in marriage?

Can divorce be justified in view of the promises made in the marriage service?

Has society made divorce too easy or too difficult?

Is marriage itself necessary or desirable? If so, is a civil or religious ceremony preferable?

Child commercials

'John is 11 years old, a fit boy with maybe a future as an athlete. He's been in care since he was a baby and naturally would like a home of his own.'

'Chris is 11. He, too, is an active, healthy boy. He'd like to live with a family and perhaps be adopted one day.'

'Mary is 6 years old and has been in children's homes all her life. She's got learning problems but a stable home would help her to overcome them.'

'Jane is 10. She's available for long-term fostering with a view to adoption but so far no one has offered a foster home.'

When four children like these were offered on television for adoption, with descriptions like the ones printed above, the television company concerned had its switchboards jammed by thousands of callers asking for more details. At the same time, the programme caused a public outcry from people who felt the children were being 'auctioned' in a tasteless way. A similar programme runs in America each week.

Finding suitable foster homes for children like John, Mary, Chris and Jane is extremely difficult, even with the help of television, for people often have the wrong motives for applying and even if they do start fostering they very often discontinue after a short time. The thousands of hopefuls who called the television company were whittled down to a mere 150 who were considered suitable potential foster parents. Social workers point out that fostering puts a tremendous stress on a home.

Critics of the programme felt it was wrong to advertise specific children who would have their hopes raised to great heights, and that the emotional atmosphere created would militate against a sober consideration by the prospective foster parents of the pros and cons of fostering.

▶ How do you feel about this type of programme? Is it the best way to attract the foster parents so desperately needed?
　Can you think of other ways of attracting more foster parents and adoptive parents?

▶ How important is it for such children to find families willing to take them on?
　Could they be better off in a well-run institution?

▶ If your group was 'vetting' prospective foster parents, what qualities would you be looking for? You could role-play these procedures.

Family ties?

The poem opposite seems fairly light-hearted but it makes a serious point.

▶ How true is the poem as a statement on human nature and the nature of families?
   Richard seems to have rejected the values of his family. How common is this? How far does the family shape a human being?

▶ Compare this poem with the story of the Prodigal Son told in St Luke's gospel, Chapter 15, Verses 11-32 (Authorised Version). How far do you think the father in this story is a model of how fathers ought to behave towards their children?

▶ 'The child is father of the man.' — William Wordsworth in *My Heart Leaps Up*.
   Discuss this assertion and its meaning.

Our brother Richard
He went his own rake-helly way;
He gamed and diced and swore.
Bred up in fear and godliness,
He loved the tavern more.

Our father drove him from the house;
We never spoke his name;
But all his trespass was our cross,
His ill-report our shame.

And if we saw him in the street,
We turned our heads aside;
And so it passed, until in rags
And poverty he died.

In life he could be none of ours;
But right is ever right.
He's buried with the family,
His faults turfed out of sight.

His grave is neat as any there;
On Saturdays we go
With roses in the summer-time,
And holly wreaths in snow.

And every Sunday praise the Lord
With calm and thankful brow,
That tidied and respectable,
We can own Richard now.

Ada Jackson

Sans everything?

... The sixth age shifts
Into the lean and slipper'd pantaloon,
With spectacles on nose and pouch on side,
His youthful hose well sav'd, a world too wide
For his shrunk shank; and his big manly voice,
Turning again toward childish treble, pipes
And whistles in his sound. Last scene of all,
That ends this strange eventful history,
Is second childishness and mere oblivion,
Sans teeth, sans eyes, sans taste, sans everything.

William Shakespeare, *As You Like It,* Act 2, Scene 7

▶ 'There are only two families in the world, my old grandmother used to say, the Haves and the Have-nots.'

Discuss this quotation from Miguel Cervantes (in *Don Quixote*) in the light of this newspaper story:

'DEATH STREET' Old folk face a cruel winter

Pensioners Michael and Sarah Metcalf go to bed at seven o'clock most nights just to keep warm. And they go without lighting to save money.

The Metcalfs, aged nearly 80, live in Gladstone Street, Newtown, where old folk living in three-room council bungalows, face another cruel winter of bitter cold and crippling fuel bills.

The old folk have dubbed Gladstone Street, 'Death Street' because of the number of fatalities brought on by the cold.

Each bungalow is heated by a single fire. Many of the pensioners have had to move their beds into the living room in an effort to keep warm.

One 78-year-old resident said: "There is scarcely a month goes by without a death. Whatever they say we know it's due to the cold, at least in part." Other residents complain of damp on walls and furniture and fittings.

The old people say that their fires are badly designed and not fitted correctly. They complain that it would cost them too much to heat the bungalows adequately.

A spokesman for Newton Council said: "We have no immediate plans to increase the heating in these dwellings. It is all a question of finance."

▶ How do you feel about the statement by the council spokesman?

▶ Discuss some of the other problems of old people and how they could be alleviated.

▶ How high a priority should we give to the needs of old people?

▶ Discuss ways you can provide help for the old people in your area. Work out detailed plans and ask your teachers if you can carry them out. It may mean finding out from the old people themselves what kinds of help they feel they need most. Perhaps go out in small groups and record their views on tape and then discuss the interviews back at school.

The following is part of a discussion between a pupil and teacher which actually took place. Paul, who is a fifth-year pupil in a comprehensive school, is arguing for Euthanasia or mercy-killing:

Paul: I think this will come in time though, compulsory Euthanasia.
T: Would you approve of this?
Paul: I would approve, yes. At a certain age, but I don't know what age that would be. It all depends on what happens in say a hundred, two hundred years' time, you know.
T: What happens if somebody was very spry at ninety-five and ninety-five happened to be the age that was fixed?
Paul: Well, if it was compulsory it would have to be carried out. I'm looking to the future now, er, centuries ahead, you know.
T: What if one of your so-called cabbages was in such a state that he couldn't express his — this is when it's voluntary — couldn't express his wish; how could you then find out, determine, what that person's wish was?
Paul: That's a good one! Well, I think then you'd have to bring the relatives in, if he had any, and if not . . .
T: Relatives who might stand to benefit from his Will?
Paul: Yes, well. That's always the case, you know. There's always somebody after something. Er, well, I think if he can't express his own will then he's got no right to live anyway, so . . .

T: It might be a temporary state.
Paul: ... if he's like a cabbage ...
T: Um?
Paul: ... if he's going to be permanently like a cabbage and he can't express any opinion at all, I think that, you know, it ...
T: Yes, but what if it's a state that's going to last for a year or two but not for ever, that he could recover ...?
Paul: Well, if there's a chance of recovery, well, there's *always* a chance of recovery, that miracle, the X factor. If it's only temporary of course he should live, but if it's going to be permanent, er, I don't think they should ...
T: There's so many imponderables here though. You're not in the realms of certainty at all, are you? Isn't this the greatest problem?
Paul: No, well, you never will be with human life.
T: Yet you're still advocating Euthanasia?
Paul: Yeah. I think it's a good thing.

▶ What do you think of Paul's views? Do you find them shocking or good sense? Discuss some of the arguments for and against Euthanasia (in the cases of the very old and the very ill) considering the following points among others:
(a) Who would carry out mercy-killing?
(b) Is Euthanasia suggested out of sympathy for the suffering of the old and ill people or a concern that resources are being wasted on them?
(c) How can we assess the quality of a life?
(d) If Euthanasia for the old became compulsory how could you fix an age for it?
(e) How could you find out the real wishes of a person who could not communicate?
(f) If relatives made the decision, could you be sure that they were not being selfish or greedy?
(g) How can you tell how permanent an illness is going to be?
(h) Might there be a danger that some people would ask for Euthanasia in a fit of depression from which they would pass in the normal way of things?

▶ Discuss the article opposite. How far do you think doctors should go in trying to preserve life?

Would you sign the Human Rights Society document?

THE RIGHT TO DIE

People who wish to be allowed to die in peace can now sign a document telling doctors not to go to excessive lengths to prolong their lives.

The document has been prepared by the Human Rights Society and it informs doctors, family and friends: "I do not want euthanasia. But if I have an incurable and fatal illness, I would prefer it to take its natural course and not be artificially prolonged. I do not want doctors to strive officiously to keep me alive or give me painful treatments which cannot succeed."

Does the family matter?

▶ Some people now question whether the family — which has been the cornerstone of our society — is really the best social unit. What do you feel in the light of your discussions thus far?

Consider other social units like a commune or Kibbutz.

Situations

The following are examples of family situations which can arise. They can be discussed without role-play, but role-play will probably lead to greater insights and give subsequent discussion more point and purpose.

1 June, who is 15, should be in by 10 o'clock. The other night, after going to a disco with some friends, she went on with them to one of the other girls' homes, and so didn't get home until just after midnight. There was a row with her parents, but, as June said to her friends the next day, "All the others were going so I had to go."

Did June have to go? Were her parents right to ask her to be in by a certain time? Would you have done the same in her place?

2 Tony is 16. He likes to play his record-player with the volume turned up and quite often he has friends in to listen to his records. His grandmother lives with the family; she is getting quite frail and is often ill. There comes a day when grandmother can stand the 'row' (as she calls it) no longer and she complains bitterly to Tony's mother, saying she will have to leave the house if her grandson carries on like this.

What should Tony's mother do? Are there ways in which it can be made easier for old people and young people to live together?

3 Linda has been warned by her parents against going about with a boy who rides a motorbike very fast and is much older than Linda. Linda's father calls him a 'layabout'. One night he is walking home from the pub when he sees his daughter on the pillion of the boy's motor cycle. When Linda gets home . . .

How do you think Linda might defend herself? What might her father say? Who is right? Are they both 'right'? Can you explain Linda's father's attitude? Should parents have views about their children's friends?

4 John is a 15-year-old who comes to stay with foster parents called Mr and Mrs Lewis. Mr and Mrs Lewis have three children of their own, Janet 17, Geoffrey 15, and Brian who is 12. John is aggressive at times and at other times he seems to sulk for long periods. Walter Lewis, particularly, likes John and strives to establish a relationship.

What sort of problems might arise? How should Mr and Mrs Lewis approach John? How do the Lewis children react?

5 Marie is 16 and her sister is 14. Liz has a habit of helping herself to Marie's make-up and Marie has warned her against it repeatedly. One morning at breakfast there is a blazing row between the sisters because Marie has just discovered that some of her eye-shadow and lipstick are missing. Their brother, who is Liz's twin, adds fuel to the fire by joining in the argument. Their parents are also drawn in.

Whom do you sympathise with and why? What should the parents do?

What other things lead to trouble between the children in a family?

Do you think rows are destructive or constructive or both?

Is it easier or harder for you to live at home now that you are a teen-ager? How do you account for this?

For further discussion

1. Should mothers of young children go out to work?
2. What kinds of rewards and punishments (if any) should be used by parents?
3. Are some kinds of parents more likely than others to have children who are delinquent?
4. What are the signs that parents care about their children?
5. The word 'love' is used a great deal. How would you define it?
6. Discuss pocket money.
7. Is there an ideal size for a family?
8. How do you feel about real commercials which use children? Do you think the children are exploited?
9. How much should children in a family contribute by taking on various tasks and chores?
10. Do people get wiser as they grow older or do they simply grow more cautious?

People at Risk

There, but for the grace of God...

globe MAGAZINE This week, feature editor Pat Smart tells the harrowing story of a nightmare life with a handicapped child

'WHAT KIND OF SOCIETY...'

Those of us who have children often grumble and grouse about the amount of time they consume and the sheer knee-weakening fatigue involved in bringing them up. But the story of John and Margaret Maxwell should make us more likely to count our blessings.

Their son Thomas is a severely subnormal and autistic child of 11. His stormy tantrums, which amount to what John Maxwell calls 'a reign of terror' mean that no one in the house can relax for a minute until an exhausted Thomas falls asleep.

When the mood takes him, Thomas quite simply goes berserk, breaking furniture and crockery, pulling down pictures from the wall, and hurling himself about in frightening fashion until finally restrained. If the Maxwells could give all their time to Thomas life would be more bearable, but they have two more children to consider, girls aged four and six.

"They are terrified," says Mrs Maxwell, "I'm really worried at the psychological harm to them of living on their nerves day in and day out. They're both developing nervous symptoms. The teachers have remarked on it with Tracy, the six-year-old."

Thomas demands constant attention. He has no control over bowels or bladder. At 11, he is physically quite strong and a real handful for Margaret when her husband is at work. There have been times when she has wished him dead.

"The damage to all our lives is so great. And we've been told he is likely to get more violent. I don't know how to face the future."

John Maxwell told me frankly of the harm Thomas had done to his marriage. "We are both under such pressure that it's not surprising that we react by blaming each other. And there is such a heavy load of guilt. We feel so negative towards Tom sometimes and then hate ourselves for feeling that way. Our family life is crumbling bit by bit. We feel utterly on our own."

The Maxwells told me they had tried over 50 institutions of one kind or another but not one would give Thomas a place. "We know we can't cope much longer and yet there seems no alternative," Margaret told me. "It's like living on the edge of a volcano. Anything can happen at any moment. You can't live with that kind of pressure indefinitely. We know Thomas should be in care and yet we can't get him in. What kind of society is it that leaves you to cope with a problem like that on your own?"

▶ Who should look after children like Thomas? Should it be the parents' responsibility?
Should they be given help? The story opposite indicates one possible form of help. Can you think of others?
Should such children be looked after in a local authority home or hostel, or in a foster home?

▶ Could there be any rewards and benefits for parents in bringing up handicapped children?
Do the Maxwells present too gloomy a picture?

▶ Do we care enough as a society about handicapped people?

Mums offered a break

Newtown mothers with handicapped children are being offered a four-hour break by a town centre play group.

Mothers and their handicapped children will be picked up at home by special bus and taken home two hours later — and this twice a week.

The children will be able to play under qualified supervision while the mums enjoy a much-needed break for relaxation or shopping.

Parents warned on child sterilisation

A REPORT out today claims that mentally handicapped children are sometimes "voluntarily" sterilised at the request of their parents.

The report, entitled "A Human Condition", says: "As mentally handicapped persons increasingly come to live in a normal heterosexual environment, the likelihood of parenthood increases.

"Anxious parents, thinking that they face a choice between institutionalising their intellectually subnormal offspring or exposing them to the supposed risk of parenthood, look upon sterilisation as the solution to their problems.

"What is often ignored, however, is the severe or even traumatic impact of an irreversible sterilisation on mentally handicapped persons," continues the report written by Larry Gostin, the Legal and Welfare Rights Officer for M.I.N.D. (National Association for Mental Health).

His report analyses the 16 years since the passing of the Mental Health Act 1959.

Under 16

He points out that Health Minister Dr. David Owen, had revealed that 38 teenagers, four of them under 16, were sterilised in 1973 and 1974.

Two of the most frequently stated public justifications were that geneticists could predict the birth of children who would inherit genetic defects and mentally handicapped parents would be unable to raise the child properly.

Referring to the "considerable controversy" on whether doctors and geneticists could make accurate predictions. he says even if they could "this still does not prove that sterilisation is appropriate."

The decision required a subjective choice of values—and the choice lay outside the expertise of doctors or geneticists or the competence of the nearest relative, "who may desire that the sterilisation takes place for reasons of self-interest," states the report.

Mr. Gostin argues that if society wishes to allow sterilisation of potentially unfit patients, the criteria for unfitness must be more specific.

▶ Discuss this news item.

Should handicapped people be allowed to have children?

If so, in what circumstances?

Should parents be able to 'volunteer' their children for sterilisation at quite a young age?

If society allows sterilisation, who should make the decision whether to sterilise or not?

What are the possible dangers in allowing the sterilisation of 'potentially unfit parents'?

What are the possible benefits to society?

How much should we care?

▶ You are starting a telephone service for the lonely and desperate.

Discuss the techniques you would use on the telephone to calm and help people under stress. Role-play some incidents and test out the techniques.

One word of advice; try to *listen* sympathetically at first and encourage the caller to keep talking rather than offering 'instant solutions' to his problem.

Before you begin, you may like to think up some 'case studies'; e.g. A 15-year-old girl rings up because her parents are making her home a hell by their bitter quarrelling and threats to split up. Sylvia is caught between the two and each tries to use her as an ally. She is approaching the crucial stage of her schooling and can't concentrate on her work. One night, when she feels particularly desperate and alone, she phones saying, 'I don't suppose you deal with *my* sort of problem, but . . . '

Accident and death

Out, out—

The buzz saw snarled and rattled in the yard
And made dust and dropped stove-length sticks of wood,
Sweet-scented stuff when the breeze drew across it.
And from there those that lifted eyes could count
Five mountain ranges one behind the other
Under the sunset far into Vermont.
And the saw snarled and rattled, snarled and rattled,
As it ran light, or had to bear a load.
And nothing happened: day was all but done.
Call it a day, I wish they might have said
To please the boy by giving him the half hour
That a boy counts so much when saved from work.
His sister stood beside them in her apron
To tell them 'Supper'. At the word, the saw,
As if to prove saws knew what supper meant,
Leaped out at the boy's hand, or seemed to leap —
He must have given the hand. However it was,
Neither refused the meeting. But the hand!
The boy's first outcry was a rueful laugh,
As he swung toward them holding up the hand
Half in appeal, but half as if to keep
The life from spilling. Then the boy saw all —
Since he was old enough to know, big boy
Doing a man's work, though a child at heart —
He saw all spoiled. 'Don't let him cut my hand off —
The doctor, when he comes. Don't let him, sister!'
So. But the hand was gone already.
The doctor put him in the dark of ether.
He lay and puffed his lips out with his breath.
And then — the watcher at his pulse took fright.
No one believed. They listened at his heart.
Little — less — nothing! — and that ended it.
No more to build on there. And they, since they
Were not the one dead, turned to their affairs.

Robert Frost

▶ What does the poem tell us about the attitudes of people to accident and death? Discuss the last two lines in particular. How do you think Robert Frost feels about death?

Discuss the Christian view of death as a beginning rather than the end.

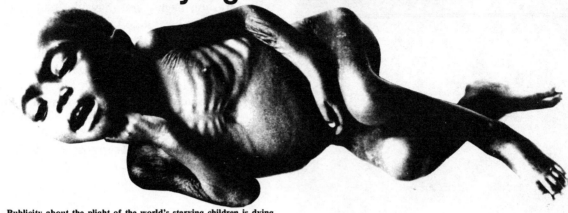

While you're eating between meals he's dying between meals.

Publicity about the plight of the world's starving children is dying down. But their problem is greater than ever. All over the world children are dying for want of food.

For food, we need money. For money, Save the Children is looking to you.

Give what you can now. Or leave it to us in your will. Your money can never buy anything more precious than a child's life.

Save the Children

'No man is an Island, entire of itself; every man is a piece of the Continent, a part of the main.

Any man's death diminishes me, because I am involved in Mankind; And therefore never send to know for whom the bell tolls; it tolls for thee.' — John Donne in *Devotions*

▶ In the light of the above quotation, how do you react to this advertisement?

Should we help people in other countries?

Should we concentrate on helping the needy in our own country?

Is there money for both?

Are problems like the one referred to in this advertisement simply 'acts of God' or could they be avoided?

'What kind of society?'

▶ Our Society has been called: the sick society; the affluent society; the permissive society. Discuss the appropriateness or otherwise of each of these labels.

Having discussed some of the questions in this chapter, do you feel we can be called a 'caring society'?

This country is, nominally at least, a Christian country. Do we live up to that name? Should we even try?

▶ Should 'charity' be organised by the state or left to private enterprise?

▶ How much is there in the argument that people suffering misfortune usually bring it upon themselves?

Situations

1 Pat, who is still at school, has her sixteenth birthday party. She has a lot of friends in and the party gets rather wild. At this point her parents return home and turn Pat's friends out. Pat is furious and sees this as the last straw. She packs a few things in a bag and leaves home later that night. She hitches a lift to London and arrives just as it's getting light . . . How might the story continue?

2 Sandra is a very shy girl who wears spectacles and suffers from asthma. She finds she is bullied at school by a group of older girls, led by one called Beryl, and her life becomes a misery. What should Sandra do? Why do people like Beryl bully?

3 Mrs Benson lives next door to Mrs Long who has three very young children and no husband at home. Mrs Benson often hears crying from next door and sometimes sounds which suggest that the children are being beaten. She sees bad bruising on Liza, Mrs Long's eldest girl. Mrs Benson is very reluctant to report Mrs Long but she is very worried about the safety of Mrs Long's children. What should Mrs Benson do?

4 Ruth is very lively girl of fifteen. She goes to lots of parties with her 'set' from the Youth Club and from school. At one party her boyfriend Mark, whom Ruth likes a lot, reveals that he has been taking drugs and he offers Ruth some tablets. Mark is very persuasive about their good effects and the lack of risk involved. What should Ruth do?

Discuss drugs in general and particular, and the attitudes of society to them. Is it right, for instance, that alcohol should be a socially acceptable drug, and that tobacco, a proven killer, should still be accepted?

5 William More is a 17-year-old who feels the values of society are totally misguided. He decides to 'drop out' and adopt an alternative life style. He meets up with some other young people who are about to begin a commune in an apparently idyllic rural setting. Role-play some possible early experiences of the group. What are their problems? Their successes and failures?

For further discussion

1. Is it too risky for young people to go on holiday without their parents?
2. Should people hitch-hike?
3. What would you consider to be over-protective behaviour on the part of parents?
4. Do we make enough provision in public places for handicapped people?
5. Ask your teachers to arrange a visit to a home for mentally handicapped children. When you return, discuss the quality of care you have seen.
6. Discuss a publicity campaign for bringing home to people the plight of starving people in other countries. Can you think of any dramatic ways of persuading people to do something about it?
7. What do you think of the work of organisations like Alcoholics Anonymous?
8. Do you think people who try to help others in distress are altruistic or do you see them as 'do-gooders' with suspect motives?

Group Life

A feeling of belonging?

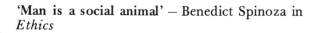

'Man is a social animal' — Benedict Spinoza in *Ethics*

'Other people are quite dreadful. The only possible society is oneself' — Oscar Wilde in *An Ideal Husband*

A comprehensive school class suggested the following list of groups people could belong to:

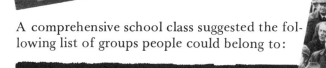

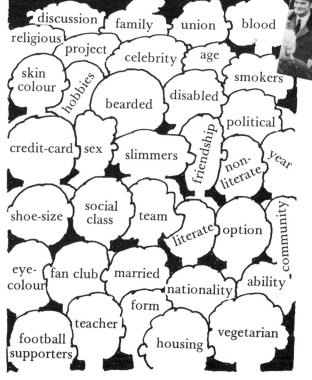

discussion, family, union, blood, religious, project, celebrity, age, skin colour, hobbies, bearded, disabled, smokers, credit-card, sex, slimmers, friendship, political, non-literate, year, shoe-size, social class, team, literate, option, community, eye-colour, fan club, married, nationality, ability, form, teacher, housing, vegetarian, football supporters

▶ Obviously some of these groups are more important than others, both in bringing people together and in driving them apart. In discussion, try to decide which are the more important groupings and say why they tend to unite people and drive them apart at the same time. Suggest other groups which exist in school or in society at large.

Taking the school groups from the list, which are most important to the teachers and which are most important to the pupils?

Why and how do groups form? What do people get from belonging to groups? In what ways can groups benefit society? In what ways can groups be dangerous to society?

Vandals rule O.K?

Anti-social groups

The vandals

▶ Look at the newspaper cuttings opposite. Notice how the vandals affect other people. Are we becoming apathetic about vandalism? Do we do enough to stop it? Do we care enough? Do the Police do enough to deter and catch vandals? What makes people 'vandalise' property? Is it a 'group activity'? Are vandals groups we can identify or are we all potential vandals?

ROWDIES' 'CLOSE TIES'
WHAT HAVE squatters, football hooligans and violent street demonstrators got in common? The answer, according to Mr. William Hirsh, is that they are all untidily dressed and do not wear ties. Mr. Hirsh, chairman of the Tie Manufacturers' Association, produced his theory at the association's annual meeting in London today.

Rail vandals 'risk a major smash'

Vandals make old folk wait for homes

Council hits at people who turn blind eye

VANDALISM: APATHY CHARGE CAUSES ROW

Vandals hit blaze rescue

The soccer hooligans

After a visit to Belgium by a British team, which resulted in some 'fans' appearing in court, a Belgian prosecutor said: 'The image of the British is of drunken youngsters throwing cobbles, bottles, and wielding sticks.'

▶ Do we deserve this reputation? What happens in groups of football supporters which leads to violence? How far is on-the-field behaviour to blame? Discuss possible steps that might be taken to cut down on hooliganism.

▶ Discuss team games. Do they help to foster co-operation and friendship or do they encourage aggressive and destructive group feelings and behaviour?

Them and us

Role-playing

Using the list of groups for ideas, role-play a situation where two rival groups clash. Show how the tension builds up between them and how individuals are caught up in the group feeling.

Divide into groups. Think of a situation (again use the list for help if you wish) where the feelings of anger or aggression in a group are turned against a person or people who are seen as outsiders. Change round and adapt the scene each time so that each of you feels what it is like to be under 'group pressure'. Discuss your feelings at the end of this. How has it added to your understanding of what happens in groups?

My parents kept me from children who were rough

My parents kept me from children who were rough
And who threw words like stones and who wore torn clothes.
Their thighs showed through rags. They ran in the street
And climbed cliffs and stripped by the country streams.

I feared more than tigers their muscles like iron
And their jerking hands and their knees tight on my arms.
I feared the salt coarse pointing of those boys
Who copied my lisp behind me on the road.

They were lithe, they sprang out behind hedges
Like dogs to bark at our world. They threw mud
And I looked another way, pretending to smile.
And I longed to forgive them, yet they never smiled.

Stephen Spender

▶ How do you think the writer feels about the boys he describes? His feelings are quite complicated. What makes groups of young people feel different in this sort of way? Is it their parents' attitudes?

Do you think young people should be encouraged to mix with people from different backgrounds or stay in groups with the same way of life?

Group power

Which group would be most likely to influence you in making the choices below:

	Parents	Teachers	Classmates	Friends
Whether or not to stay on at school				
Choosing new clothes				
Whether or not to smoke				
Whether or not to go on a school trip				
Choosing a career				
Where to go for your holiday				
Which subjects or options to take at school				
Whether or not to be in the school play				
Whether to work hard or fool about at school				
Whether to do homework				

▶ Discuss your answers with the others in the group.

▶ In many situations a group can achieve a great deal that an individual could not achieve on his own. After all, that is the thinking behind this book in suggesting that the group works together. Here are some situations where groups of people work together:

    A trial
    A planning committee
    A union meeting
    An interview
    A school council.

Think up some situations for these groups to consider and role-play what happens. Think each situation out in detail, and perhaps circulate each person taking part with written material so that certain important facts are established at the beginning.

▶ What do you think about the conflicting views on the subject of school uniform voiced in readers' letters opposite?

YOUR LETTERS

SCHOOL UNIFORM

"uncomfortable and unsuitable"
"nothing smarter"

Sir—
I think the move against school uniform is part of a general decline in standards. There is, to my mind, nothing smarter than the traditional school uniform and it gives pupils pride in themselves and their school. It also has the great advantage of making pupils from well-off homes and those from poorer homes look indistinguishable — a point that should appeal to the disciples of egalitarianism and equality. If only these young girls who are so keen to get into the latest fashions realised it they look far more attractive in their uniforms. I used to love to see smart boys and girls getting on my bus wearing uniforms, and could tell which schools they were from.

Must we abandon all our traditions and standards because of pressure from a vocal minority of 'progressives'?

B.S. Edinburgh.

Sir—
I agree wholeheartedly with the criticisms of school uniform in your last issue. Why should our children be forced to wear a mode of dress which anyway is often uncomfortable and unsuitable for the work they do, just because schoolteachers want conformity? Dress is after all an expression of individuality and personality. Why do we seek to deny the right of self-expression to school-children? It seems to me that uniform is part of the old public school tradition which is hardly relevant to life in today's comprehensive schools with their cosmopolitan and generally heterogeneous populations.

L.R. Portsmouth.

Sir—
We are often told that uniforms look smart and that they hide differences in the social backgrounds of the wearers. Both points are nonsense. Uniforms can look tatty like any other form of clothing and the pupil from the deprived home may wear a uniform of sorts but it may well be his brother's hand-me-down or it's through at the sleeves.

M.B. Leeds.

Sir—
I'm sure many of the critics of school uniform are not mothers of adolescent girls. I wonder if they realise the commercial pressures on young girls to follow the ridiculous vagaries of fashion in dress generally and in shoes in particular. Schools which insist on uniform do the parents a great favour. It is far more economical to buy a uniform than it is to keep buying the latest 'gear'. And there is a strong argument in favour of uniformity on the grounds of safety alone. Some of the footwear worn by the girls is positively lethal on the open staircases which are common in the new schools.

F.C. Wrexham.

Sir—
I cannot see what all the fuss is about over school uniform. As I understand it, few schools are rigid on this matter as in the past. It is common now for schools to allow a wide range of acceptable dress — usually in certain specified colours — including trouser suits and the rest. As long as they guard against the really way-out gear they are happy.

Q.N. Liverpool.

▶ How far should schools go in expecting conformity on such matters as dress, hair styles, wearing of jewellery, etc.?

Is it part of a legitimate attempt to build up group identity?

Prejudice?

'O wad some Pow'r the giftie gie us
To see oursels as other see us!' — Robert Burns
in *To a Louse*

▶ Consider national groups.
What kind of person is the typical

    American
    German
    Japanese
    Frenchman
    Italian?

Give evidence to support your views.

What generalisations are often made about the British? Are people from the four countries of the United Kingdom very different in 'national characteristics'?

▶ In what circumstances are nationalism and patriotism good or bad?

Easily led?

NEWTOWN HIGH SCHOOL

NAME .. John Lewis ....
FORM .... 5.As .... Spring .. TERM

SUBJECT	GROUP	GRADES	REMARKS	Teacher's Initials
ENGLISH	B	A- B+	A very good term's work. John has done useful work as a librarian.	
HISTORY	B	C- D	John is easily led and allows himself to be distracted by others in the group.	

▶ After discussing some of the questions in this section, how do you feel about the influence of group attitudes and group feeling? When is group influence positive and when is it negative? In what sort of situations should you stand up for your own opinion and when should you compromise?

Leaders of all kinds have used groups to get and keep power. How? Is it true to say that groups get the leadership they deserve? Do groups need leaders?

Situations

1 Mark is apprehensive about his first day at Comprehensive school. He has heard about the 'initiation ceremony' for new boys. At break he is caught by a group of fourth-formers who begin the initiation . . .

Four years later Mark's group catches a new first-year boy called Brian and begin the initiation ceremony. Mark sees the youngster's obvious distress and remembers his own discomfort four years ago.

What should he do? What do you think about initiation ceremonies? Can you think of any other groups that initiate new members? Why do they have these rituals?

2 Class 4X at Newtown Comprehensive school is not very well-behaved with certain teachers. They discover that a girl in their class called Mildred has gone to the Deputy Headmistress to inform about some of their escapades. How do you think the class would react? How would they treat Mildred? How should they treat her? How do you feel about Mildred's action? Do you think there are times when loyalty to the group should come second to some other consideration or should it always come first?

3 The Lowsons live next door to a house which is for sale. An Asian family moves in; the first immigrant family to come to live in the street. How should the Lowsons behave towards their new neighbours? What might happen to influence the Lowsons?

4 Imagine your group is the staff of a brand new school. You are holding a staff meeting to draw up a list of rules for the new school. 'Appoint' a Headmaster first if you wish to or you may be completely democratic and give every teacher equal power. What, if any, rules are you going to have?

5 You are the new manager/coach of a soccer/hockey team and you find your team seems to lack team spirit. What would you do to improve this? Discuss different possibilities. Role-play some of the situations where you bring members of the team together to try to improve things. One problem is that one of the team thinks he/she should be the manager/coach.

For further discussion

1. Do we encourage too much competition in schools?
2. Is there sexual equality in schools?
3. How can large schools be organised to help pupils to feel that they belong?
4. What do you think of the behaviour of pop group audiences?
5. What do you think about the arguments for greater devolution of power in Britain?
6. How far do you think you change as a person, as you move from group to group?
7. What happens in your group discussions? Do the same people tend to dominate? Are certain people looked to for leadership? Do people sometimes get heated? Do you think those who don't speak still get something out of the discussion? Do you ever change your mind as a result of what someone says in discussion?
8. Can you work out together ways to help those groups of people who are ill or disabled? Think of services or entertainments you could provide for people in a local hospital. This could be performing a play, for instance, or making toys for children or acting as disc-jockeys on the hospital internal radio — or a host of other possibilities.

   Obviously you need to discuss your plans with the hospital staff at a fairly early stage.

Power and Authority

Power structures

Most organisations and institutions have a hierarchy. The power pyramid below represents the organisation of a fairly typical Comprehensive school. It is likely that your school is similar.

▶ Discuss this way of distributing power and responsibility.
What are its advantages and disadvantages? Is it efficient?

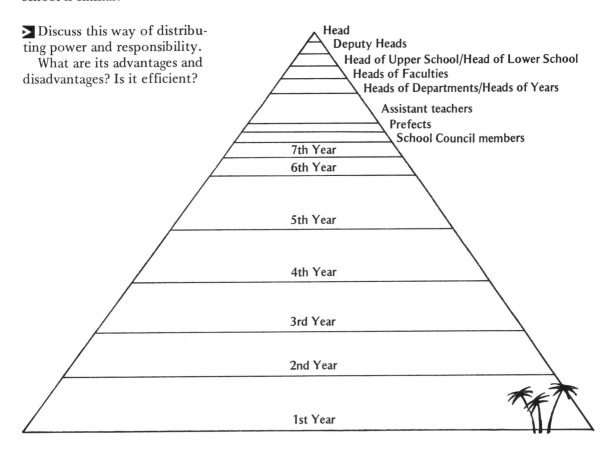

▶ Can you think of other possible ways of organising schools?
How much power and responsibility should be in the hands of the pupils?

▶ Is the power pyramid the best model for organising
a) the country, b) industry, c) the Armed Forces?

Discuss some other possible models. Perhaps the circle shape suggests a different way? Can you think of other shapes or models?

How much freedom?

Read this account of life in a very different school from the 'typical' school illustrated by the power pyramid on the previous page. This is one person's view of Summerhill, a school run by the late A. S. Neill. At this boarding school children were given the freedom to attend lessons or not as they wished, and any 'rules' were made by the children and teachers together in a democratic meeting.

Children in the grounds of Summerhill

How does Summerhill work? What does it do, and how? What is the secret of Neill's art? . . .

Over the years, many children have gone to Summerhill who were wholly defeated and demoralised by life, locked in their desperate protective strategies of self-defence and deliberate failings, filled with fear, suspicion, anger, and hatred. I knew one such child myself. Only a year before he went to Summerhill, he seemed not far from a complete breakdown. At Summerhill he got well. Most of the children there — not all, the school has had its failures — get well. They get back their strength, confidence, and courage, and turn to face life and to move out into it, as all healthy children really want to do, instead of running and hiding from it. In a school that does not care much about schoolwork many of these children, hopeless failures in school after school, begin to do competent and even excellent work, often progressing two, three, and even five times as fast as conventionally good students in conventionally good schools.

What else in the school helps children to get well? Children there do many things that most adults, in home or at school will not let them do — swear, be dirty, wear raggedy clothes, break things. At the meeting I went to, a girl of about twelve contentedly sucked her thumb throughout the meeting, taking it out now and then to make some astute comment. Nobody teased her or seemed to take any notice. Is there something intrinsically therapeutic about being able to use four-letter words, or go for days without a bath? I doubt it. What seems more important is that these children were freed from the enormous pressure under which they had been living. For many of them, life before Summerhill must have seemed one long battle, most of it against adults whose love or goodwill they needed and wanted. A hundred times a day they must have had to face the agonising decision: shall I do what Mother or Father or Teacher or Authority tells me, or not? What do I stand to gain? What to lose? These are not light calculations. Having to make them day after day must be exhausting to children as it would be to many of us. They had to spend so much time and energy either doing or not-doing what others told them to do that they had no time and energy for doing things on their own. One way or another they were always reacting to others, giving in or resisting, but in neither case acting independently, autonomously, pursuing their own interests and needs.

From *Freedom and Beyond* by John Holt

> What do you think of the ideas behind this school? Do you think children should have freedom from the 'agonising decision: shall I do what Mother and Father or Teacher or Authority tells me, or not?' Do you think you would welcome freedom or would you be afraid of it? Could state schools be run on the lines described here? How much freedom and choice is right for young people of your age? Do you think pupils could and should run a school or do you think the teachers would be abdicating responsibility if they didn't make the decisions?

Role-playing

Set up a moot or school council and let it deal with the following cases:
- a boy who has been stealing;
- a boy who has been bullying;
- a girl who disrupts lessons;
- a teacher who is accused of inefficient teaching and not marking work.

Powers of persuasion

Role-play the following situations with crowd reactions (where appropriate):
- persuading people to buy in an outdoor market;
- swaying a crowd against its leaders (cf. Mark Antony's speech in *Julius Caesar*);
- justifying a declaration of war;
- a candidate for a school council appealing for votes;
- trying to persuade people in slum properties that it is in their interests to stay;
- trying to persuade people in slum properties that it is in their interests to move;
- a door-to-door salesman selling encyclopaedias or double-glazing;
- a Headmaster justifying the introduction of compulsory uniform, regular homework and the use of the cane in a school which has not had these in the past.

Crime and punishment

> Consider this collection of newspaper headlines. In treating criminals, should the primary purpose be retribution or reform?

Hospital for girl who stole baby

New Sentences for offenders

THIEF TO 'WORK' FOR COMMUNITY

HANGING — NEW MOVE IN THE COMMONS

Courts 'too easy' on salmon poachers

SERVICE INSTEAD OF JAIL

VIOLENT CRIME FIGURES SOAR

Are the courts too easy on offenders?
Should people who commit crimes be regarded as sick?
Is community service by offenders a good idea?
What other methods of dealing with criminals could be tried?
Should corporal punishment be used for certain offences?
Discuss the arguments for and against capital punishment.

Discuss the times when *you* have broken the law or done things which have harmed or hurt other people. What led you to do these things? Does this give you any insight into the ways in which we should treat wrongdoers?

Retribution or reform?

'Some of us may die'

The poem below tells us a lot about the power and powerlessness of the state. Discuss how it does both:

Your attention please

The Polar DEW has just warned that
A nuclear rocket strike of
At least one thousand megatons
Has been launched by the enemy
Directly at our major cities.
This announcement will take
Two and a quarter minutes to make,
You therefore have a further
Eight and a quarter minutes
To comply with the shelter
Requirements published in the Civil
Defence Code — section Atomic Attack.
A specially shortened Mass
Will be broadcast at the end
Of this announcement —
Protestant and Jewish services
Will begin simultaneously —
Select your wavelength immediately
According to instructions
In the Defence Code. Do not
Take well-loved pets (including birds)
Into your shelter — they will consume
Fresh air. Leave the old and bed-
ridden, you can do nothing for them.
Remember to press the sealing
Switch when everyone is in
The shelter. Set the radiation
Aerial, turn on the geiger barometer.
Turn off your Television now.

Turn off your radio immediately
The Services end. At the same time
Secure explosion plugs in the ears
Of each member of your family. Take
Down your plasma flasks. Give your children
The pills marked one and two
In the C.D. green container, then put
Them to bed. Do not break
The inside airlock seals until
The radiation all clear shows
(Watch for the cuckoo in your
Perspex panel), or your District
Touring Doctor rings your bell.

If before this, your air becomes
Exhausted or if any of your family
Is critically injured, administer
The capsules marked 'Valley Forge'
(Red pocket in No. 1 Survival Kit)
For painless death. (Catholics
Will have been instructed by their priests
What to do in this eventuality.)
This announcement is ending. Our President
Has already given orders for
Massive retaliation — it will be
Decisive. Some of us may die.
Remember, statistically
It is not likely to be you.
All flags are flying fully dressed
On Government buildings — the sun is shining.
Death is the least we have to fear.
We are all in the hands of God,
Whatever happens happens by His Will.
Now go quickly to your shelters.

Peter Porter

▶ What do you think of the lines:
 'We are all in the hands of God,
 Whatever happens happens by His Will'?
 How successful is this broadcast as propaganda?

▶ Do you think this country should continue to have nuclear weapons or do you think we should disarm?

▶ Can a Christian justify the use of force? Consider these words spoken by Christ:

Ye have heard that it hath been said, An eye for an eye, and a tooth for a tooth: but I say unto you, That ye resist not evil: but whosoever shall smite thee on thy right cheek, turn to him the other also . . . . .
Ye have heard that it hath been said, Thou shalt love thy neighbour, and hate thine enemy. But I say unto you, Love your enemies, bless them that curse you, do good to them that hate you.

St Matthew, Chapter 5, Verses 38-44
(Authorised Version)

▶ Could people live by this teaching? Could countries live by this teaching? Is there such a thing as a 'just war'? Can 'appeasement' be dangerous?

Here are two verses from a poem by Thom Gunn called 'Klaus Von Stauffenberg' about the German officer who tried to kill Hitler in a bomb-plot in 1944.

In this case, did the end justify the means? Was Von Stauffenberg right to use force against Hitler or was he placing himself on the same level as Hitler by attempting to use force to destroy him?

▶ Do you think peaceful resistance can work?

The maimed young Colonel who can calculate
On two remaining fingers and a Will,
Takes lessons from the past, to detonate
A bomb that Brutus rendered possible.

Over the maps a moment, face to face:
Across from Hitler, whose grey eyes have filled
A nation with the illogic of their gaze,
The rational man is poised, to break, to build.

Power of direct action

More and more groups of people are taking direct action to change things they don't like or to impose their will.

Examples are squatting, sit-ins, and demos, and, more violently, taking hostages and hi-jacking.

▶ What do you think of these actions? Are some more justified than others? Is there too little respect for the rule of law in this country?

Power corrupts?

▶ Having discussed some of the issues in this chapter, how far do you agree with Lord Acton's famous statement: 'Power tends to corrupt, and absolute power corrupts absolutely. Great men are almost always bad men.'

▶ Do you think politicians in this country exercise power responsibly? Benjamin Disraeli said: 'I repeat . . . that all power is a trust — that we are accountable for its exercise — that, from the people, and for the people, all springs, and all must exist.'

How far do politicians behave as though they recognise the truth of this statement? Is there enough power in the hands of ordinary men and women?

Situations

1 The police surround a squat in a large house and give the squatters, led by 'Honest Joe', an ultimatum to be out by ten o'clock the next day. Joe, appearing at an upstairs window, shouts down a speech justifying the squat. What might he say?

The police return the next day and find the squatters still occupying the building. What should the police do? Role-play what happens.

Earlier, a lady called Mrs Lee had written a letter of complaint to a local newspaper on the subject of the squatters. What do you think she would complain about? Do you sympathise with her?

2 Role-play a hi-jacking incident. Try it with at least two different endings. Discuss at the end what you have discovered about the ways people behave in this sort of situation. Who had the most power?

3 Linda Bellamy is a 17-year-old worker in a stocking factory. She becomes the central figure in a dispute which leads to a strike. Role-play the events of this dispute and how it is resolved. Again, discuss who appeared to have most power. How true-to-life do you think the situation was?

4 Marcia Hughes, 16, had an illegitimate baby who was adopted. After the adoption, Marcia found she missed her baby terribly. One day she found herself taking a baby from outside a supermarket . . . .

What might happen from this point in the story? If Marcia is caught, how should she be treated?

5 Re-read the poem 'Your attention please'. Role-play some of the scenes which might follow the broadcast. Would all of the broadcast be obeyed? Would every family have a shelter? What might happen at the shelters? What might happen inside the shelters? Would leaders emerge? How would they get and keep power?

6 In the book *Lord of the Flies,* by William Golding, a group of boys who were flying in an aircraft which is shot down, find themselves on an island without any adults. What do you think would really happen in this situation? Role-play some incidents.

For further discussion

1. Examine the sanctions against bad behaviour which are normally used in schools: lines, detentions, the cane, etc. Which are most effective? Can you think of any more effective methods of promoting good behaviour?
2. What are the advantages and disadvantages of a Prefect system in a school?
3. How much truth is there in the saying: 'Spare the rod and spoil the child'?
4. 'Make love, not War'. Discuss.
5. How do you feel about conscientious objectors?
6. Have the Trade Unions in this country got too much power?
7. Could Britain become a totalitarian state?
8. Should we continue as a monarchy or is there a superior system for Britain?
9. Try to make a number of visits to courts. When you get back to school discuss what you think of British justice in action.

Man and Beast

For good or ill?

SMOKING DOGS AND SHAMPOOING RABBITS

How animals suffer for our lipsticks, shampoos and deodorants

Animal lovers in Britain are becoming increasingly concerned at the way animals are being used in experiments.

They cite the recent experiments carried out in ICI laboratories, where beagles were made to 'chain-smoke' in order to help scientists devise a safer cigarette for humans. Opponents are angry that dogs should develop smokers' coughs and suffer other ill effects in what are essentially non-medical experiments.

And how does it happen that shampoos are deliberately put into the eyes and on the skin of rabbits partially encased in plaster of paris to prevent them scratching it off? This is done in the interests of developing safe cosmetics to satisfy the vanity of the human species. Animal lover groups believe these non-medical experiments should be banned by law. Others, including some scientists who are mounting a pro-vivisection campaign, emphasise the importance of making cosmetics, food additives and agricultural chemicals safe for humans and believe there is no alternative to using animals.

Cancer link pills withdrawn

Two birth control pills, taken by about 75,000 women in Britain, are being withdrawn following discoveries that one of the hormones they contain produces tumours in the breasts of beagle bitches.

The move to withdraw the pills comes after American Scientists found evidence that beagle bitches fed up to four times the human dose of the hormone, megestrol acetate, continuously over a period of seven years, developed tumours, of which some were cancerous, in their breasts.

This contrasts with other progestogen hormones used in other pills which produced no increase in breast tumours in similar trials in the United States.

▶ Discuss these cases of animals being used in experiments.

Is the suffering caused too high a price to pay for progress in developing safe cosmetics, cigarettes and drugs?

Are some of these experiments more justified than others?

Is there a case for using human beings rather than animals in some or all experiments?

Are there any other methods available to the scientists?

Does the anti-vivisection position reveal a sentimental attitude to animals?

For fun?

The British Union for the Abolition of Vivisection has provided these statistics about bullfighting in Spain.

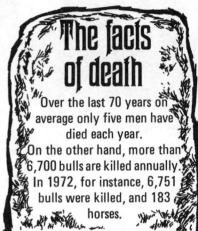

The facts of death
Over the last 70 years on average only five men have died each year. On the other hand, more than 6,700 bulls are killed annually. In 1972, for instance, 6,751 bulls were killed, and 183 horses.

▶ Discuss your feelings about bullfighting in the light of these statistics.

Is any cruelty involved outweighed by the magnificence of the spectacle and the bravery of the bullfighter?

It is said that bullfighting in Spain might die out if it was not in great demand by tourists, many of them British. Should the tourists boycott bullfights?

▶ How do you feel about other so-called 'blood-sports'?

Oscar Wilde called fox-hunters: 'the unspeakable in full pursuit of the uneatable'. Do you agree, or do you think fox-hunting is an effective method of pest control?

What do you think of the tactics some groups use to disrupt fox-hunting and hare-coursing?

Fishing is said to be the most popular sport in Britain. Does it involve cruelty?

▶ Discuss other ways in which we use animals to provide us with fun and spectacle: zoos, circuses, horse-racing, horse-jumping, greyhound-racing, etc.

The following poem by Ted Hughes describes a number of animals in a zoo:

The Jaguar

The apes yawn and adore their fleas in the sun.
The parrots shriek as if they were on fire, or strut
Like cheap tarts to attract the stroller with the
    nut.
Fatigued with indolence, tiger and lion

Lie still as the sun. The boa-constrictor's coil
Is a fossil. Cage after cage seems empty, or
Stinks of sleepers from the breathing straw.
It might be painted on a nursery wall.

A caged panther

For food?

Is the following poem fair to farmers?

Harvest Hymn

We spray the fields and scatter
The poison on the ground
So that no wicked wild flowers
Upon our farm be found.
We like whatever helps us
To line our purse with pence;
The twenty-four-hour broiler-house
And neat electric fence.

All concrete sheds around us
And Jaguars in the yard,
The telly lounge and deep-freeze
Are ours from working hard.

We fire the fields for harvest,
The hedges swell the flame,
The oak trees and the cottages
From which our fathers came.
We give no compensation,
The earth is ours today,
And if we lose on arable,
Then bungalows will pay.

All concrete sheds ... etc.

John Betjeman

But who runs like the rest past these arrives
At a cage where the crowd stands, stares, mesmerized,
As a child at a dream, at a jaguar hurrying enraged
Through prison darkness after the drills of his eyes

On a short fierce fuse. Not in boredom —
The eye satisfied to be blind in fire,
By the bang of blood in the brain deaf the ear —
He spins from the bars, but there's no cage to him

More than to the visionary his cell:
His stride is wildernesses of freedom:
The world rolls under the long thrust of his heel.
Over the cage floor the horizons come.

▶ Does this seem an accurate description of a zoo? Does it create a favourable picture of zoos? In what way is the jaguar different from the other animals described? Why does Ted Hughes appear to admire the jaguar?

▶ Discuss some of the farming methods referred to in the poem. Do you think modern methods are unnatural and inconsiderate to animals, or essential in the interests of efficiency and economy? Why has Betjeman written this as a hymn?

▶ 'A man is what he eats' — Ludwig Feuerbach, 1804-1872.
Some people claim vegetarianism is the only civilised and responsible answer. Discuss the pros and cons of vegetarianism.

Cruelty

Arrest warrant for man who starved and chained dog

"REVOLTING PHOTOGRAPHS"

Yesterday Newtown magistrates ordered the arrest of the owner of a greyhound which chewed away half of its kennel wall, but couldn't escape because of chains fastening it to the floor.

The prosecutor said the "particularly revolting photographs" of the dog would speak for themselves. When it was found by an RSPCA Inspector, the greyhound weighed 24 lbs, a third of its normal weight.

It was described as emaciated and dehydrated, lying down and able only to raise its head. All the bones stood out prominently. A container on the floor of its tiny, badly-constructed kennel on some allotments, seemed to have only urine in it and the dog couldn't reach it as the chain was too short. It had numerous bedsores and was caked in its own dirt. There was nothing in the dog's stomach. It had to be destroyed immediately.

▶ Why do people subject animals to cruelty and neglect?

How should such people be treated by society?

Do we take on animals as pets too lightly?

Should some people be banned from keeping animals? Should the dog licence system be changed?

Do we make too much fuss about cruelty to animals and too little about, say, cruelty to children?

Do we deserve our reputation as a nation of animal lovers?

What do you think of the work of the RSPCA?

RSPCA warns of pet presents

Kindness ?

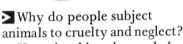

Old man hanged himself after pet budgie died, inquest told

MAN DROWNS AFTER SAVING PET PUPPY FROM RIVER

▶ Do these authentic headlines from newspapers suggest we sometimes make animals too important?

Why should some people lavish great love on animals?

In their treatment of pets, are some people cruel when they think they are being kind?

▶ What do you think of some of the animal breeding that is done today, such as the breeding of miniature dogs? Do we interfere with and manipulate nature too much?

▶ Having discussed the questions in this section, how do you feel about the way we, as the most developed animal species, exercise our responsibilities towards lesser creatures?

Situations

1 Albert Sewell leads a group of people violently opposed to blood sports. The group hears that the Longchester Hunt has a fox-hunt planned and they meet to discuss the methods they will use to try to disrupt it. Role-play their meeting and the later clashes between the demonstrators and the hunt. Bring out the arguments on both sides.

2 In *Animal Farm* by George Orwell, the animals rebel and take over their farm. Role-play a similar situation. Include a rousing speech by the leader of your animals in which the crimes of the human species are catalogued, and let the animals draw up an 'animal charter' which sets out their grievances and how their situation should be remedied. How does the revolution progress?

3 The scene is Hyde Park corner. Rudolph Fitzgibbon, flanked by various placards and posters, is a vegetarian making a strong attack on meat-eaters and the ill-treatment of animals which their meat-eating habits encourage. As he speaks he is heckled by the crowd and various arguments are used against him. Discuss the most effective slogans he could use on his placards and let different members of the group play Rudolph's role. Try to develop interesting exchanges between the speaker and the crowd.

4 David is seven years old and he has just discovered his hamster is dead. He is very upset. How should his parents, and other members of the family, deal with this situation? Role-play what happens.

5 One evening in Spring the Melvilles are surprised by a visit from the police who tell them that their dog has been identified as one which has been terrorising sheep in the area. Their first reaction is to reject completely the idea that their Kim is the culprit. What happens?

6 Act a science-fiction story in which aliens collect human beings for a zoo. What specimens are collected, and why? How are they acquired? What sort of 'zoo' would house them? What situations arise?

For further discussion

1. Discuss the many and various ways in which animals help man.
2. If in some reincarnation you could come back as animals, which would you choose to be and why?
3. Do we do enough to conserve rare species?
4. Ask members of the group to bring pets or animals to school and talk about them. Ask the speakers questions and involve the whole group in discussion.
5. Find out more about the work of such organisations as the RSPCA and the PDSA, perhaps by inviting speakers to come to talk to you. Find out their problems and whether there are any practical things your group can do to help.
6. Discuss some of the ways selective breeding and animal husbandry generally might develop in the future.
7. Discuss how far you think cruelty is involved in training animals for the circus and other entertainments.
8. Should owners of pets be subjected to greater restrictions to prevent nuisance and annoyance to people who don't like animals?

Alexander Markham, a newspaper editor, is in the studio with Radio Newtown presenter Susan Foley. The subject of the phone-in is **FREEDOM OF THE PRESS**.

Susan: We have a Mr Hart from Kent on the line. Mr Hart, what is your question to Mr Markham?

Mr H: I want to know why the press in this country can't act more responsibly.

Mr M: What do you have in mind, Mr Hart?

Mr H: The prying into people's lives and the hounding of people that goes on. People in public life have no privacy. Who wants to know details of their sex lives, anyway?

Mr M: Publication of details of people's private lives should only happen if there is a legitimate reason for revealing them. It could be in the public interest to reveal facts about someone's private life.

Mr H: I don't see how.

Mr M: Well, for instance, if a politician was making thousands of pounds out of property deals at the same time as publicly criticising others for doing the same.

Mr H: I'm thinking more of the muck-raking that goes on. And the methods used to collect some of the information that we read are very suspect, sometimes downright unlawful.

Mr M: Again, I don't know what you have in mind, but unorthodox and unlawful methods are only justified in exceptional circumstances and only if other methods are not possible. What if there is corruption or a cover-up on the Watergate scale? Then it may be possible for people in power to block the use of lawful and legitimate methods. It may be necessary to do things which are technically unlawful because this is the only way to get at the evidence you know exists.

Susan: Are you convinced Mr Hart?

Mr H: Not really. I think the press should be controlled by strict laws. Newspapers have far too much freedom.

Mr M: A free press is essential in a democracy. In fact, of course, that freedom is far from total; for instance we have the laws of libel, the Official Secrets Act, and the Government's 'D' notices.

Mr H: There should be more restraints.

Mr M: I believe strict laws on privacy would be against the public interest because reporters would find it impossible to carry out their investigation and inquiry and to be vigilant on behalf of the ordinary man and woman.

Mr H: You keep using the phrase 'in the public interest' when I think you mean 'of interest to the public' or some sections of the public. I don't doubt some people are interested in filth and trivia but that doesn't mean you've got to pander to them. Some of the photographers, for instance, have no respect for people in the public eye.

Mr M: I wouldn't defend all the actions of all newspapers. There are some bad apples in every barrel.

Mr H: That isn't good enough when we're dealing with something as powerful as the press. I'm worried, too, about the terrible bias of some papers. You get news mixed up with comment when surely they should be kept separate.

Mr M: This is a matter of policy for each newspaper. Surely you wouldn't want a law about that? Straight news can be pretty dull and people like lively comment. Anyway why shouldn't a paper have a point of view?

Mr H: But people are often unable to distinguish the news from the comment if the news is presented with a subtle slant as it often is.

Mr M: I think the public is more intelligent than you suppose.

Mr H: I think you are the people who treat the public as if they were morons, filling papers with sex and sensationalism.

Susan: Thank you Mr Hart. I think I ought to bring in another caller. Thank you again.

▶ Discuss the arguments presented here and other pros and cons on the issue of a free press.

Gutter Press

News Editor: Peer Confesses,
Bishop Undresses,
Torso Wrapped in Rug,
Girl Guide Throttled,
Baronet Bottled,
J.P. Goes to Jug.

But yesterday's story's
Old and hoary.
Never mind who got hurt.
No use grieving,
Let's get weaving.
What's the latest dirt?

Diplomat Spotted,
Scout Garrotted,
Thigh Discovered in Bog,
Wrecks Off Barmouth,
Sex in Yarmouth,
Woman in Love with Dog,
Eminent Hostess Shoots Her Guests,
Harrogate Lovebird Builds Two Nests.

Cameraman: Builds two nests?
Shall I get a picture of the lovebird singing?
Shall I get a picture of her pretty little eggs?
Shall I get a picture of her babies?

News Editor: No!
Go and get a picture of her legs.

Beast Slays Beauty,
Priest Flays Cutie,
Cupboard Shows Tell-Tale Stain,
Mate Drugs Purser,
Dean Hugs Bursar,
Mayor Binds Wife With Chain,
Elderly Monkey Marries For Money,
Jilted Junkie Says 'I Want My Honey'.

Cameraman: 'Want my honey?'
Shall I get a picture of the pollen flying?
Shall I get a picture of the golden dust?
Shall I get a picture of a queen bee?

News Editor: No!
Go and get a picture of her bust.

Judge Gets Frisky,
Nun Drinks Whisky,
Baby found Burnt in Cot,
Show Girl Beaten,
Duke Leaves Eton —

Cameraman: Newspaper Man Gets Shot!
May all things clean
And fresh and green
Have mercy upon your soul,
Consider yourself paid
By the hole my bullet made —

News Editor: Come and get a picture of the hole.
(dying)

Paul Dehn

> How far is this a fair description of the press in this country?

Is the poem revealing about human nature?

Should newspapers try to educate public taste or simply be as popular as possible in order to sell as many copies as possible?

> Bring in a selection of newspapers and analyse them in group discussion.

How much news?

What kind of news? Is it mixed with comment? Is it 'slanted'?

How many by-lines (reporters' names) and how much from news agencies?

How good is the coverage of world news?

What kind of photographs? Why are they included?

How much editorial comment?

What kind of feature articles?

How much advertising?

How good is the coverage of sport?

Does the paper have articles specifically for women? Should it?

What are your criteria for judging a newspaper? Thrash this out and then decide which paper comes out best.

> Is it healthy that newspapers are so dependent on advertising? What results does this tend to produce?

PRISONS TOO COMFORTABLE

STOP WELFARE FIDDLERS

Tied-up boy burnt in a lark, court told

Quake victims: more missing

IMMIGRANTS FAVOURED

Permission to kill?

▶ Why do you think there are so many films with themes like those advertised below?

▶ The film advertised opposite was exceptional.
It was made on a modest budget and was not expected to make much money.
If you have seen it, can you account for its success?
Discuss what makes a good film.
How far is film an art form or simply a branch of entertainment?

▶ How do you feel about film censorship?
What do you think of the present arrangements for film certification?

▶ How true do you think this statement is in relation to our attitudes to censorship:

'An Englishman thinks he is moral when he is only uncomfortable' – G.B. Shaw in *Man and Superman*.

Power of the box

Try role-playing some television interviews, imitating the techniques used by real interviewers. Choose a topic like 'freedom of the press', films, or 'the power of television' as a subject for the interview.

▶ Have television interviewers too much power?

Do they overstep the mark in interviewing politicians?

Has performance on television become too important in judging a politician's suitability for high office?

▶ Discuss the view that there is too much sex and violence on television.

How far do you agree with the attitudes of Mary Whitehouse who was first associated with the 'Clean-Up T.V. Campaign' and later with the National Viewers and Listeners Association?

▶ People are divided about the influence of television.

Does it affect people or not? Does violence on the screen lead to violence in real life?

What are its effects on family life?

Does it kill conversation?

Does it cause disagreements?

Does it encourage passivity?

Is it educational?

Do comedy programmes about colour encourage or discourage prejudice?

Decline of the Bookworm

▶ In spite of campaigns against illiteracy, people say books, and the written word generally, are becoming less and less important.

Is this true?

If so, what are the reasons?

If not, what evidence can you produce to support your view?

Would it matter if the written word declined in importance?

What use are works of fiction?

What use, if any, is the creative artist to a society like ours?

▶ Conduct a survey of people's reading habits, including books, newspapers, magazines and comics. *Choose your sample with care*. Perhaps use your school, or a particular class or group, or interview a sample of the public at large. Is it to be a random sample or a cross-section, or some other approach?

Cassette tape-recorders will help.

Enlist the help of local newsagents and local libraries.

There are various ways in which you can present your material once it is collected. Your local radio or television, if you have it, may be interested in broadcasting some of your results.

The persuaders?

Analyse these advertisements.

What is the 'psychology' behind each advertisement?

Collect others from newspapers and magazines and analyse them, perhaps in small groups. Let each group 'report' to the class as a whole.

Try to pick out the most persuasive advertisements.

Why are these more successful than the rest?

What is the use of advertising?

Read and discuss the British Code of Advertising Practice.

Are these standards strict enough?

Protectors or parasites?

▶ After discussing some of the issues raised in this section, how do you feel about the media in this country? Are the media playing an important 'watchdog' role in the best interests of our democracy and our freedom, or are they to be seen more as parasites on society, feeding off people's misdeeds and misfortunes at the same time as feeding people with pap?

Situations

1 You are 'radio reporters'. Research various 'stories' and record them on tape. Interview people with the aid of cassette recorders and use music to build up a programme. This could develop into your own school radio service if you have the necessary equipment. You will probably find that your local radio is quite willing to let you see round and get some idea of how programmes are made.

2 You are the advertising department of a well-known detergent firm. Role-play a meeting where you discuss your campaign to launch 'SPRAY' on the market. Discuss advertisements on hoardings, in newspapers, and on television, and other methods to be used to promote the product. What are the main selling points and what is the main 'angle' to be used?

3 You run a consumer protection programme on television. Devise tests and carry out research into the efficiency and value for money of various products. Choose things which matter to you as consumers: make-up, crisps, shampoos, ball-point pens, pocket calculators, etc. Let each group present its findings to the class as a whole, well-mounted and made interesting visually.

4 Lance Love is a 16-year-old boy with aspirations to be a pop star. Rupert Green elects himself his manager and gathers a group around him who are determined to make Lance 'top of the pops'. Role-play meetings of this group. How can you get Lance noticed? What is his 'gimmick'? How will you keep him in the public eye? How will you stage-manage his public performances?

5 You are a team of television people who make documentaries which 'take the lid off' various aspects of life. You want to make a programme about a comprehensive school. Take your own school and discuss how you can show it in its best possible light. Then imagine your team of reporters is anti-comprehensive and discuss how you could make a programme which would show the worst aspects of your school. If you have VTR equipment and a camera in school, or you can borrow the equipment from a teachers' centre, consider making the actual programmes.

For further discussion

1. How far do you think teenagers are exploited by the media?
2. How do you feel about horror comics and war comics? Are they harmless?
3. Why are certain regular serials on television ('soap operas') so popular? What methods are used to keep an audience viewing?
4. Collect and analyse some of the advice given on the 'problem pages' of magazines. What do you think of it?
5. Do you think people can be corrupted by pornography?
6. What do you feel about 'access radio and television' which is meant to let ordinary people use the media? Is this an idea which should be developed?
7. Discuss how local radio can make a positive contribution to the life of an area. Send some of your best ideas to your local radio station.
8. Arrange for the girls in your group to examine comics and magazines written for boys and vice versa. Come together and discuss your findings.

Questions of Belief

I believe...

The following are extracts from the writing of comprehensive school pupils invited to write about their beliefs.

'I believe in a life before this one. This is why you think that you've been here before.'

'I don't believe in black magic or even the devil. I believe everybody has a bit of evil in them but some more than others. Some people can't control this evil and this is the devil to me.'

'When you see all these disasters on the news I sometimes wonder if there is a God.'

'I don't believe in the healing Jesus is supposed to have done, making crippled people walk and deaf people hear and blind people see. I think this is just a fairy story.'

'I believe that Jesus was not the son of God. My belief is that he was just a very good doctor and had a very good knowledge of medicine and knew the proper treatment for some of the diseases which nobody else knew.'

'I believe in God and a life after death. When you are buried your bones stay underground but your soul goes to heaven and then the Lord makes your soul into something else.'

'I believe in Communism. They have built Russia into one of the strongest countries in the world. Communism has made some of the most advanced countries from some of the most backward.'

'I don't believe in good luck.'

'I believe that when I am playing a game with my friends if I don't step on a line on the pavement, it will bring me good luck but if I step on the lines, it will bring me bad luck.'

'I believe that twins can communicate. If one of the twins is suffering the other twin can feel that there is something wrong.'

'I believe you can make yourself ill because of worrying about something.'

'I believe in acupuncture because people who have had operations with acupuncture say they haven't felt a thing.'

'I believe that dreams can foretell the future.'

'My mother has warned me never to play with a ouija board and if I do I will regret it all my life.'

▶ Discuss these statements. They raise many issues, for instance telepathy, psychosomatic illness and alternative medicine, as well as the existence, or otherwise, of God.

'Opium of the people' ?

'Religion . . . is the opium of the people.' — Karl Marx in his introduction to *Criticism of Hegel's Philosophy of Right*.

▶ Is religion, as Marx suggests, like a drug, which makes life less painful and more bearable? Marx implies men should be able to live without it. What do you think?

Consider these words spoken by Jesus Christ:

And he said to them all, if any man will come after me, let him deny himself, and take up his cross daily, and follow me. For whosoever will save his life shall lose it, but whosoever will lose his life for my sake, the same shall save it. For what is a man advantaged, if he gain the whole world, and lose himself, or be cast away?

St. Luke, Chapter 9, Verses 23-26 (Authorised Version)

... and he opened his mouth, and taught them, saying,
Blessed are the poor in spirit: for theirs is the kingdom of heaven.
Blessed are they that mourn: for they shall be comforted.
Blessed are the meek: for they shall inherit the earth
Blessed are they which do hunger and thirst after righteousness: for they shall be filled.
Blessed are the merciful: for they shall obtain mercy.
Blessed are the pure in heart: for they shall see God.
Blessed are the peacemakers: for they shall be called the children of God.
Blessed are they which are persecuted for righteousness' sake: for theirs is the kingdom of heaven.
Blessed are ye, when men shall revile you, and persecute you, and shall say all manner of evil against you falsely, for my sake. Rejoice, and be exceeding glad: for great is your reward in heaven: for so persecuted they the prophets which were before you.

St. Matthew, Chapter 5, Verses 2-12 (Authorised Version)

▶ Does this sound as easy a way as Marx implies?

Is it an ideal which is impracticable or could men live by this teaching?

What differences would it make to a person's life? What sort of situations would they get into?

How would your school change if everyone lived according to the teaching of Christ? Would the changes be an improvement?

How would our society change if everyone lived by this teaching?

Why are the qualities listed by Christ in the Sermon on the Mount not more valued in our society?

'... by their fruits ye shall know them'

▶ What is R.S. Thomas saying about the Church in the poem opposite? Are the implied criticisms justfied?

▶ How far do you think the various Churches live up to the example of Christ?

▶ Should the Churches be concerned about the relatively small number of people who are members? Why are their memberships small?

Do you think they should try harder to attract more members? How could they do this?

▶ Should the Churches be involved in politics?

▶ What do you think of the 'hard sell' methods used by some religious groups?

▶ Do you think Churches should have hierarchies?

▶ Should women be allowed to join the clergy?

In church

Often I try
To analyse the quality
Of its silences. Is this where God hides
From my searching? I have stopped to listen,
After the few people have gone,
To the air recomposing itself
For vigil. It has waited like this
Since the stones grouped themselves about it.
These are the hard ribs
Of a body that our prayers have failed
To animate. Shadows advance
From their corners to take possession
Of places the light held
For an hour. The bats resume
Their business. The uneasiness of the pews
Ceases. There is no other sound
In the darkness but the sound of a man
Breathing, testing his faith
On emptiness, nailing his questions
One by one to an untenanted cross.

R. S. Thomas

Clever devils?

'Educate men without religion and you make them but clever devils.' — attributed to Arthur Wellesley, Duke of Wellington, 1769-1852.

▶ What do you think of this quotation? Should religion form a part of everyone's education? If so, what form should the teaching take? If not, should anything be put in its place?

▶ What do you think about school assemblies?

▶ What is the purpose of 'moral education'? Are morals caught or taught?

Feeble minds?

'Superstition is the religion of feeble minds.' — Edmund Burke in *Reflections on the Revolution in France.*

THIS WEEK LARA, GLOBE'S STARGAZER SUPREME, DOES AN

In depth horoscope for

CANCER JUNE 21 — JULY 20

This week all you cancer children are under very benevolent influences with only Thursday likely to cause the odd ripple on a smooth pond. Put to sea for the week's voyage on Sunday with weather set fair for both work and play. At work, particularly, this could be a very successful week, not so much financially but in terms of relationships with your shipmates. In a week like this your best qualities tend to show, so make the best of it. You have leadership qualities and although everyone can't be captain of the ship, everyone can help to keep it on course.

▶ Discuss astrology and other attempts to predict the future.
   Why are such things so popular?
   Have they any validity?

▶ Is 'civilised man' more superstitious than he imagines?
   Discuss Burke's view of superstition.

▶ Can man discount the supernatural completely?

From vampires, witches and werewolves...

'From ghoulies and ghosties and long-leggety beasties, and things that go bump in the night, Good Lord deliver us!' — old prayer from Scotland.

Today interest in black magic, witchcraft, and the occult generally, is said to be very widespread.

▶ What is the fascination of the supernatural?
Are people looking for a substitute religion?
Is interest in these things unhealthy?

▶ Do you believe people can be 'possessed'? If so, is this a matter for the Church or the medical profession? If not, how do you account for apparently para-normal behaviour such as faith-healing or 'miracle cures' or people committing murders apparently under the influence of evil possession?

Mind over matter ?

Meditation is good for you!

A Way of Coping with Tension and Stress

Yoga and other forms of meditation are catching on in a big way all over the world. A report recently revealed that the United States Air Force had asked an Indian guru to supply teachers of meditation to all its bases.

In Britain, too, thousands are now turning to meditation as a way of achieving inner peace and better mental health.

For many people simple techniques are involved, requiring only, say, twenty minutes twice a day; elaborate physical positions are not necessary although they may help those who wish to take it further.

Misconceptions

There are many misconceptions about meditation. It is not a religion and does not lay down a moral code for its devotees. The people who indulge are not all bearded cranks or grimy dropouts.

Many people are living conventional lives and use meditation to cope with tension and stress and to achieve greater self-discipline, training body, and, particularly, mind to a high pitch of performance.

Techniques vary but can be very simple and natural, sitting with your eyes closed to aid concentration. A particular sound, a 'mantra', is repeated with a quality which allows your nervous system to settle down. The effect of this is to assist you to shut out the world and your personal preoccupations and achieve stillness and peace.

Teachers of mediation point to the dangers of people experimenting with meditation without fully knowing what they are doing. And one snag: lessons in meditation are often rather expensive.

But champions of meditation, including some very famous people, are more than enthusiastic about its good effects. In one small town in Britain even a drop in crime figures was attributed to the high number of people in the community practising meditation.

▶ Discuss this newspaper article.

Do you believe techniques like these work?

Do you believe the mind controls the body?

Do you believe in faith healing?

How do you account for the growing numbers of people turning to Yoga and other mental and physical disciplines of a similar kind?

How free is free ?

▶ Western Europe and America are often referred to as 'the free world'. How free are we?

Discuss democracy as a political system.

▶ People are often referred to as 'free agents', meaning that we have choices about how we behave: But in view of some theories in psychology, how free are we?

What about the influences of heredity and environment?

▶ A banner bearing this inscription was held aloft at the 1976 Cup Final. After discussing some of the issues in this chapter, do you feel men need something to believe in?

Can you explain the popularity of 'substitute religions'?

Do we pay enough attention to the spiritual side of man? How far is man a rational creature?

Have we anything to learn from other cultures in satisfying the spiritual man as well as the physical and rational man?

Situations

1. Alfred Simcox is the new vicar in Lazenby Parish, Newtown. He is young and has many ideas for making his Church more lively and relevant, including some changes he wants to make in some of the actual services. He discusses his ideas with a small band of workers. What might these changes be? How does the group react? What happens?

2. Organise a 'mock election' with selection of candidates, preparation of manifestos, speeches and campaigns, interviews with the media, and the final voting and count. Use the normal political parties or perhaps invent parties such as 'the campaign for the liberation of the British schoolboy or girl.'

3. In the chapter on 'Power and Authority' we referred to the book *Lord of the Flies*. What are the most basic beliefs that these boys should try to live by on their island? Discuss them and try to hammer out a list of, say, six of the most basic, essential 'rules' if anarchy and death are to be avoided.

4. Fred Sinclair will not join the rest of his colleagues in staging a strike over an issue he does not believe in. What methods do Fred's colleagues use to try to bring him into line? Role-play some of the incidents which follow.

5. Role-play the following:
Choose from your group a panel of 'clergy' from different Churches and denominations and let them answer questions from the audience, i.e. the rest of the group. Perhaps write questions down on slips of paper and have a chairman select them from a hat and put them to the speakers. The 'clergymen' should try to respond as they think a representative of their Church would answer. Later discuss the differences in belief which emerge. Can you account for some of the differences? Is it good or bad that Christianity is represented by so many different denominations?

For further discussion

1. Should priests be celibate?
2. To what do you attribute the upsurge of interest in the martial arts and other aspects of Eastern cultures generally?
3. How far is our education system a form of indoctrination?
4. Why are religious groups often so intolerant of one another?
5. What do you think about spiritualism and other attempts to contact the dead?
6. As a follow-up to Situation 5 above, invite representatives of different denominations into school as speakers and discuss your questions with them.
7. In small groups investigate local Churches and report back on what each Church contributes to the life of the community.
8. Discuss agnosticism. Is there a sense in which everyone must be an agnostic?

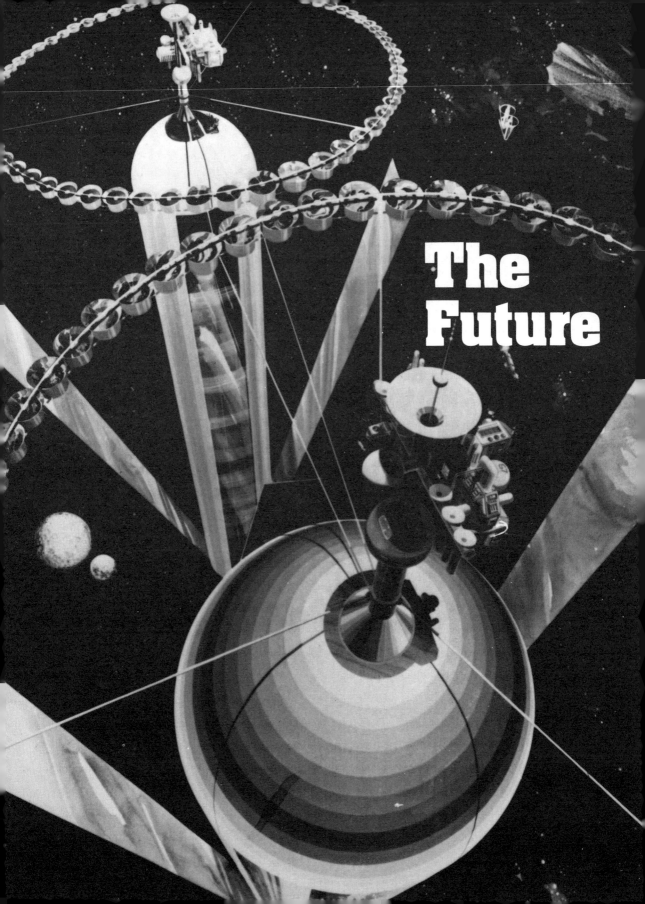

Futurology?

This could be part of a school timetable of the future.

4f	Technology	Computer Studies	Environmental Studies	Futuro
4g	Human Movement	Futurology	European Studies	Outdoo
4h	Creative Arts	Astronomy	Communications	Recrea

▶ What about the rest of the timetable?
Could these be the subjects studied in schools of the future?
What other subjects might be studied? Why?
How will education be organised in the future?
What will education be for?

▶ Discuss the following:
We study History but there could be a stronger case for studying the future, in the sense that intelligent predictions and planning are essential in a complex society like ours. There are many examples of things going drastically wrong because of a lack of intelligent foresight.

But consider this statement by Edmund Burke:
'You can never plan the future by the past' —
(Letter to a member of the National Assembly)

'Here again are the main points of the news'

You are invited to play the futurology game in the rest of this section.
A comprehensive school class suggested these items for a news broadcast for the year 2500.

'Mr Voskavitch, representing the Russia-Africa-Americas alliance, has arrived in London for disarmament talks with the European-East Federation.'

'Today the Superbeings established their exclusive right to another profession, that of Urban and Rural Planning.'

'Council today gave a final reading to the Bill making it compulsory to carry a fire-arm for personal protection.'

'The Bank Holiday rush began this evening with flights to the moon fully booked.'

▶ Discuss the thinking behind these predictions. How likely are they?

▶ Discuss each area, e.g. political developments, 'class' or social divisions, violence, and space travel, in your own way, e.g. political developments:
what is our political future?
what new 'power blocks' will arise?
will countries learn to co-operate through organisations like the U.N?
what about so-called 'underdeveloped' countries?
will conflicts grow between black and white peoples?

Doomsday + 365

Is this the scenario for the future?

The Horses

Barely a twelvemonth after
The seven days' war that put the world to sleep,
Late in the evening the strange horses came.
By then we had made our convenant with silence,
But in the first few days it was so still
We listened to our breathing and were afraid.
On the second day
The radios failed; we turned the knobs; no answer.
On the third day a warship passed us, heading north,
Dead bodies piled on the deck. On the sixth day
A plane plunged over us into the sea. Thereafter
Nothing. The radios dumb;
And still they stand in corners of our kitchens,
And stand, perhaps, turned on, in a million rooms
All over the world. But now if they should speak,
If on a sudden they should speak again,
If on the stroke of noon a voice should speak,
We would not listen, we would not let it bring
That old bad world that swallowed its children quick
At one great gulp. We would not have it again.
Sometimes we think of the nations lying asleep,
Curled blindly in impenetrable sorrow,
And then the thought confounds us with its strangeness.
The tractors lie about our fields; at evening
They look like dank sea monsters couched and waiting.
We leave them where they are and let them rust;
'They'll moulder away and be like other loam.'
We make our oxen drag our rusty ploughs,
Long laid aside. We have gone back
Far past our fathers' land.

And then, that evening
Late in the summer the strange horses came.
We heard a distant tapping on the road,
A deepening drumming; it stopped, went on again
And at the corner changed to hollow thunder.
We saw the heads
Like a wild wave charging and were afraid.
We had sold our horses in our fathers' time
To buy new tractors. Now they were strange to us
As fabulous steeds set on an ancient shield
Or illustrations in a book of knights.

We did not dare go near them. Yet they waited,
Stubborn and shy, as if they had been sent
By an old command to find our whereabouts
And that long-lost archaic companionship.
In the first moment we had never a thought
That they were creatures to be owned and used.
Among them were some half a dozen colts
Dropped in some wilderness of the broken world,
Yet new as if they had come from their own Eden.
Since then they have pulled our ploughs and borne our loads,
But that free servitude still can pierce our hearts.
Our life is changed; their coming our beginning.

    Edwin Muir

> Discuss the poem.
  What do you think made the world that has been destroyed 'that old bad world'?
  Why do the horses represent a new beginning?

> Develop in role-play the idea used by Edwin Muir in his poem.
  What happens to your group of survivors as they pioneer a new beginning?
  Act out a series of incidents which show their problems, their triumphs, and their setbacks.
  There may be other groups of survivors who do not share your views about how things should be organised.

S-F?

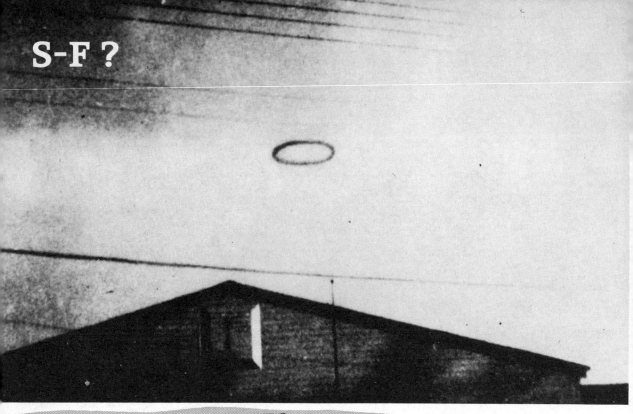

We saw cigar-shaped UFOs...

THREE Oldtown schoolboys want to know if anyone else saw two UFOs in the sky above Oldtown.

They are very embarrassed because no one believes their story. "The other lads think we're crackers," said Mark Letts, 14.

Coming out of Oldcroft School at the end of the day, they heard a loud buzzing noise.

When they looked up they saw two cigar-shaped objects like flying saucers. The boys, Dennis Mulvaney, 14, Malcolm Smith, 13, and Mark, were walking across the yard when they saw the mysterious objects. "We couldn't believe our eyes," said Dennis, "They were like you imagine flying saucers to be but more of an elongated shape."

▷ How do you react to stories like the one above?
What do you think of the likelihood of life-forms on other planets?

▷ Discuss some of the science-fiction you have read. (Perhaps include writers like H.G. Wells, Ray Bradbury, and John Wyndham.)
What do you think of this kind of fiction? Do you think any of these stories contain credible predictions of the future?

▷ Discuss some possible ideas and plots for science-fiction stories.
Again, some of your ideas may lend themselves to development in role-play and drama.

Take some present trends and discuss how they might develop in the future. You might take things like popular music and pop culture, fashion, food, leisure pursuits, and transport, but there is a host of possibilities.

One giant leap for mankind?

Astronaut Walter Cunningham photographed during the flight of Apollo 7.

▶ Having played the futurology game a little, are you pessimistic or optimistic about the future?

What do you think the quality of life will be in, say, the year 2000?

What about work? How far will automation go? What will be the contribution of computers and robots? How will people be rewarded for work?

Will mankind have taken the giant leap forward of eliminating poverty and starvation? Will co-operation replace competition at international level?

Will mankind still pursue material prosperity and economic growth as ultimate goals?

Will there be a place for religion and worship? Will there still be a place for the priest and the parson?

How will the young be brought up?

What will be our attitude to the old and infirm?

Look back through this book and consider how our attitudes to some of the issues raised may change in the future.

Situations

1 Colonel Zin is the leader of a Venusian expedition to earth with a mission to explore and report on the earthlings' civilisation. As members of Colonel Zin's expedition, discuss and compose your report on man today, as anthropologists might report on a newly-discovered tribe or culture.

2 Hector Russell is a politician campaigning in the year 2010. Discuss the political issues with which he is concerned. One plank in his platform may be a campaign for equal rights for men.

3 Your group is a group of historians set the task of writing a history of Britain in the 1970s. Discuss the areas you will include in your book and try to sort them into some order of importance.

4 Your group has acquired a few acres of land and a certain amount of capital and you wish to design a dwelling which is self-sufficient in terms of energy and amenities. Discuss how this home and small community will be designed, built and organised.

5 Again, the year is 2010. You are a group of town planners planning a new town centre. Discuss what amenities and facilities you will provide.

For further discussion

1. Do you consider the money spent on space exploration by the Americans and Russians was well spent or should it have been put to other uses?
2. Do you think man can control the pollution problem or will he ultimately poison his own planet?
3. How do you think medicine might develop in the future?
4. Do you see George Orwell's predictions in *1984* coming true?
5. Do you think the inequalities in our society will finally disappear and, if so, will this mean a general levelling up or levelling down of standards?
6. Could undersea communities exist in the future?
7. What changes in climate might occur in the future and with what results?
8. How do you think the human species will continue to evolve in the future?